EDUCATION MATTERS

DAVID ABBOTT

EDUCATION MATTERS

Need2Know

LIGHTING THE WAY TO A GOLDEN FUTURE

First published by Need2Know 1997
Need2Know, 1-2 Wainman Road, Woodston,
Peterborough PE2 7BU

Edited by Kerrie Pateman
Typesetting by Forward Press Ltd

Contents

Introduction

What this book will do for you

The aim of this book is to show you how to help your children get the best education possible. Many people are unhappy with the education their children get, but don't say anything about it. Sometimes this is because they just feel that they can't do anything about it, sometimes it's because they don't know what they can do about it, and sometimes it's because they are frightened to try and do something about changing things.

This book will help you understand today's education system and get the best from it.

The bad news

We live in a time when good jobs, job security, and a good standard of living are becoming increasingly hard to obtain.

Work is much more stressful and competitive, and periods of redundancy are now becoming a common experience for more and more people. Obviously we want something better for our own children, and most concerned parents know that the best start a young person can get is the best possible education.

For many parents, school was a long time ago, and they may be bewildered by the variety of new subjects and schools available. If we also take into account the large number of *experts* who are frequently seen on TV disagreeing with each other it is no wonder that parents may be confused.

In addition to this, education is discussed with a great deal of technical jargon, which many find hard to understand. GCSE, GNVQ, Attainment Targets, Ofsted, Level of Attainment, SATs, UCAS, and so on. Parents can frequently feel that this is designed just to confuse them.

'...be sure to visit these desks before you leave - GNVQ, Ofsted, SATs, UCAS, GCSE, Statementing, Attainment Targets, SCAA, LEA...'

Despite what politicians and media may say at times, there are excellent educational opportunities for all who want them badly enough. Once you have a basic understanding of how the system works and how to deal with those working in the education system, you are in a position to start making the system work for you.

Don't believe anyone who tells you that the solution to getting the best out of the education system depends on 'contacts' or knowledge which is only open to the select few. Anyone can gain the knowledge which will enable their child to succeed.

How to deal with schools

Perhaps more important though for many parents is dealing with teachers, schools and educational jargon. This book will certainly help you in dealing with all these things to get what you want for your child, showing you how to choose a school, what to look for in a good school, how to check that your child is making progress, and how you can help.

You will also find lots of advice on finance, school trips and activities, legal matters, coping with exams, and careers and higher education advice. Once you have this knowledge you should be confident that you will be able to do the best for your children.

1 UNDERSTANDING THE EDUCATION SYSTEM

- Who runs the education service?
- Types of school
- The Education system
- What types of Private Education are available?
- Your rights and responsibilities
- Summing up...

Education in the United Kingdom has recently undergone many changes. The creation of the National Curriculum, regulating the subjects which must be taught throughout the country, has brought many administrative changes with it. Schools are now required to provide more information to parents on a variety of issues including attendance and exam performance. In addition there have been changes to the way schools are governed and managed. The first step in understanding the new system, then, is to answer the question 'Who runs the education service?'

Who runs the education service?

Education is provided free by the government for all children between 5 and 16 and up to 19 for those taking their education beyond the minimum leaving age.

This service is run by the Secretary of State for Education and Employment, who is appointed by the Prime Minister.

The Secretary of State is responsible for making government education policy, approving plans for the National Curriculum, organisation and quality of teacher training, educational standards, and has powers to close schools if standards are deemed unsatisfactory.

The Secretary of State is helped in this by the Civil Service Department for Education and Employment who administer government policy.

Other Government bodies
In addition there are several other bodies affiliated to the government which report to the Secretary of State.

- SCAA
- OFSTED
- Local Education Authorities

SCAA
The School Curriculum and Assessment Authority, is responsible for overseeing the content (what is taught) of

the school curriculum and testing, and for monitoring standards and syllabuses of public examinations, such as GCSE and A Level.

Ofsted

The Office for Standards in Education, organises the inspection of schools, and its work is overseen by Her Majesty's Inspectors of Schools (HMI). Education policy in Scotland, Wales and Northern Ireland, is determined by the Scottish Secretary, the Welsh Secretary, and the Secretary of State for Northern Ireland, respectively.

Local Education Authorities

Local Education Authorities (LEA's) are usually organised on a county or metropolitan borough basis. Each LEA will consist of an Education Committee of elected councillors, who will formulate policy and be aided in implementing policy by a Chief Education Officer, or a Director of Education. National education policy is set by the government and the Secretary of State for Education and Employment, but LEA representative and officials are responsible for ensuring that there is adequate provision for all eligible within the authority's area. In effect this means that LEA's are responsible for transport, Special Educational Needs, grants, allocating school places at primary and secondary level, information on schools and some aspects of budgets for schools.

Governors
Within each school, responsibility for the everyday running lies with the Board of Governors.

The Governors are collectively responsible for issues such as appointing staff, discipline, budget and sex education.

The Headteacher is frequently a member of the board of Governors, although this is not a necessary arrangement.

Regulations regarding the number of governors vary according to the size of the school. Boards of Governors usually include parent governors, teacher governors, LEA appointed and some co-opted members (invited / picked by existing Governors).

Who runs Education? - Summary
- Secretary of State and Department of Education and Employment
- Local Education Authorities
- School Governors
- Head teachers

Types of school

Governance
Schools can be categorised in terms of the way they are run, and in terms of who runs them. One important distinction to establish at the start is that between schools provided by the state, referred to as maintained schools, since it is the Government which maintains them, and

independent schools, generally called private schools. Independent or private schools can set their own entry examinations and requirements, and charge fees.

Maintained and voluntary schools

There are two types of maintained school, county schools and voluntary schools.

County schools which include primary and secondary schools, are those schools which are funded entirely by the LEA.

Voluntary schools are those schools which have a different relationship with the LEA - this usually means that some proportion of the financing of the school or the ownership of the property was contributed by some voluntary (ie non-governmental) body.

Frequently in Britain this means the church, and there are many Church of England or Roman Catholic Voluntary Aided schools.

Other types of school

Governance

What are grant-maintained (GM) schools?

Grant-Maintained schools were initiated by the 1988 Education Reform Act. All primary and secondary schools are able to apply to the Secretary of State for Grant-Maintained Status.

Grant-Maintained status means that the school is no longer

funded by the LEA, but receives its funding directly from the Government.

This is known as 'opting out', meaning that a GM school has opted out of LEA control.

There are currently around 1000 GM schools in the UK.

GM status may be attractive to schools because the funding, in all respects similar to local authority levels, includes an extra 15% (for a limited period).

Many commentators have seen this as a way to encourage schools to opt-out of local authority control. Opting-out will be discussed in more detail in Chapter 2.

City Technology Colleges

City Technology Colleges (CTC's) were initiated in 1986, with the first college opening in 1986. CTC's were intended to provide secondary education with an emphasis on technology and business in the curriculum. They were aimed at inner city areas, and intended to provide more choice for parents (more about CTC's later).

CTC's are mainly funded by the state with additional help from industrial sponsors. Hence, some CTC's are named after well known companies.

CTC's are not administered or funded by local authorities.

CTC's have not developed as rapidly as the government expected, partly because it has been difficult to find companies willing to offer sponsorship. There were 14 CTC's in 1995.

Types of school - summary

- Maintained schools
- Voluntary schools
- Independent schools
- Grant maintained schools
- Special schools

The Education system

A brief outline of the way in which the education system is governed has been given in the previous pages. We now need to focus on the smaller elements in the system - the schools themselves, in order to see how education is organised at the grass roots.

How are primary schools organised?
Primary schools in the UK generally provide an education for children aged between the ages of 5 and 11. Children usually start primary school in the year of their fifth birthday. Primary schools are usually co-educational, teaching boys and girls, though private schools are more often single-sex. Some schools provide nursery provision for children under 5.

What will children be taught in Primary schools?
Primary schools are now required to teach the National

Curriculum.

Primary school pupils will therefore study English, Maths, Science, Music, Technology, Geography, PE, Art and History (there will be more about the National Curriculum in Chapter 2).

The class watched attentively as Wolfgang performed *Eine Kleine Nachtmusik* before offering their criticisms

You will find a variety of teaching styles in primary schools, depending on the subject being taught and the particular task being undertaken.

Pupils will be taught for most of the time by one teacher, their class teacher, but the specialist demands of the National Curriculum may mean that they have specialist teachers more frequently than was the case prior to the National Curriculum.

How will children be taught in Primary schools?
Much of the work at the primary stage may be done as project work. This may mean that the teacher will organise a project on for instance, grass. Work can then be done in many of the subjects mentioned, using the topic of grass as an interlinking theme. Thus children can write poems about grass (English), study its growth (Maths and Science), design equipment to cut grass (Technology), and so on.

How are secondary schools organised?
The British education system has changed gradually since the Second World War, and there are a variety of types of secondary school, catering for the 11-19 age range. All these schools have to teach the National Curriculum.

Comprehensive schools are the most common type of school throughout England, and cater for all abilities, and are usually co-educational. As they cater for all abilities, Comprehensive schools will teach academic and vocational courses.

Despite the many changes in the education system there are still around 150 Grammar schools remaining. Grammar schools put great emphasis on academic achievement, and operate selective entrance policies. Selection to Grammar school can be very competitive.

There are also secondary modern schools, which tend to be less academic and focus more on practical subjects.

All the above types of secondary school will generally take in pupils at 11. Some schools will not have provision for pupils beyond 16, but most Comprehensive schools and

Grammar schools will have a sixth form. In many parts of the country though provision for the 16-19 age range is made available through specialist sixth form colleges, which teach a variety of academic and vocational (training aimed at particular jobs, eg car mechanic) courses. Additionally there are Colleges of Further Education throughout the country which provide a similar range of courses, but which generally focus more on vocational provision.

Is Secondary schooling organised in the same way throughout the country?

There are some additions to these main types of provision. The most important are those local authorities which organise provision in terms of First Schools (5-9), Middle Schools (9-13) and Upper Schools (13-19). The age bands indicated here may vary slightly in different local authorities. This arrangement does not alter the curriculum, children in such schools will be taught the same National Curriculum subjects as children in Primary and Secondary schools throughout the country.

Education in Scotland and Northern Ireland

Educational provision in Scotland is provided through the Regional and Island councils. There are three types of school; those run by the Regional council are called public schools, and there are also grant-aided schools, and independent schools. Grant-Aided schools are funded by the Scottish Office, and have a status roughly the same as GM schools in England and Wales.

In Northern Ireland education is run by Education and Library Boards. Again there are three types of school; controlled schools, voluntary grammar schools, and independent schools.

There are some differences in what is taught in the different parts of the UK (see Chapter 2).

What types of Private Education are available?

Private schools (independent schools) range from the most well known public schools, to private day nurseries.

Montessori and Steiner schools, for instance, offer an education based on a particular view of how children learn.

Other schools cater for particular religious beliefs; there are Roman Catholic, Quaker, and Muslim schools for example.

There are also private schools which emphasize particular aspects of education, eg sports, academic, music, etc.

Some parents may choose a private school because they want a traditional and single sex school. For others, their lifestyle may necessitate sending their child to boarding school, a service mainly available only from private schools.

Private schools do not have to teach the National

Curriculum, though many do. They receive no funding from the government and charge fees. Private schools must be registered with the Department for Education and Employment.

There are a limited number of Assisted Places at some 300 independent schools. Further information can be obtained from the Independent Schools Information Service (see Help List).

Your rights and responsibilities

You have a right for your child to receive a free education between the ages of 5 and 16, and up to 19 if they decide to stay on beyond minimum leaving age. On the other hand, you are legally required to ensure that your child receives an education between 5 and 16, and if registered at a state school, you are responsible for your child's attendance. You do not, however, have to use the state education system. As mentioned before, you have the choice of private education, or you may wish to opt for educating your child at home. You do not need to be a qualified teacher to take this last option, but you will need to show the authorities that your child is receiving an appropriate education - which means an education which they feel is right given your child's age and ability.

Summing up...

There is a wide range of different types of school to choose from. Now that we have had a look at how the education system is run, it's time to take a closer look at schools and examine what they teach.

2 THE 1988 EDUCATION REFORM ACT & THE NATIONAL CURRICULUM

- The National Curriculum
- Core and Foundation subjects
- Key stages
- The National Curriculum and testing
- Open enrolment
- Opting out
- Summing up...

The National Curriculum

The National Curriculum was brought into effect by the 1988 Education Reform Act. The Act also had important effects on the way schools were run and established in law. Schools were obliged to provide parents with certain information about the school's performance in general, how parents could follow through any complaints, and what information parents should get about their child's progress.

For some the National Curriculum is to be seen as unnecessary meddling in education by Government, which has only had the effect of burdening students with too much testing, and teachers and schools with too much bureaucracy.

There may well be some truth in this criticism. On the other hand, the National Curriculum does offer parents the assurance that their children have received the same educational opportunities as other children in the state system, through a basic curriculum taught to all.

Whilst the National Curriculum may present many advantages for parents and students, it does make it important for parents to have a basic knowledge of what subjects are in the curriculum, as well as a grasp of the terminology used in the National Curriculum. As mentioned, the government legislation which brought in the National Curriculum has also led to changes in the way schools are run and funded. Schools now have the option to 'opt out', and the rules about enrolment - which schools your child can go to, have been changed. This chapter aims to equip parents with sufficient knowledge of these changes to make informed decisions about their child's education.

Core and Foundation subjects

The National Curriculum consists of Core and Foundation subjects. The Core subjects are the subjects seen to underlay all further education beyond 16 years of age.

Core subjects: English, Mathematics, and Science.

Foundation subjects: Art, Geography, History, Modern Languages, Music, PE., and Technology.

What will my child have to study?
The Core subjects have to be studied by all pupils up to the age of 16, whilst there is some room for flexibility with the foundation subjects, since pupils may choose options from 14, when most GCSE courses begin.

Most pupils may find that they drop a subject or two at 14. Students may find for instance that they can study either Geography or History, or Integrated Humanities up to GCSE, but not all three.

Key stages

The subjects outlined above are designed to be taught to all children throughout the period of their compulsory schooling. This has led to some changes in the way we refer to various stages in a child's education.

Many parents may be familiar with the numbering of the primary school years, eg first, second, third, and fourth year, with transfer to secondary school at age eleven at the end of the fourth year.

Secondary schools may likewise be remembered as starting with the first year and ending with the sixth form.

The new system
These year designations have now been replaced with a chronological system.

Education may last thirteen years, starting at 5 and ending at 18 after A levels.

Thus children now commence their education in Year 1, and proceed to Year 11 (GCSE year), and may opt to continue their secondary education to A levels, completing their studies in Year 13.

In devising the National Curriculum, the Government felt that a child's education could be divided into a number of key stages. The National Curriculum is therefore organised in a number of key stages for the purpose of arranging what is to be taught and testing what children should have learnt. There are four key stages, as indicated in the table:

KS	Ages
1	5-7
2	9-11
3	11-14
4	14-16

You may often see these stages referred to as, for example, KS1, KS2, etc, on reports or at parents evenings.

Assessment and Standard Assessment Tasks (SATS)
An important part of the motivation in devising the National Curriculum was to ensure not just that certain subjects and topics were taught, but also to build in regular testing and monitoring of student achievement into a new system.

The National Curriculum and testing

There has been considerable debate between teachers and the government as to whether the National Curriculum tests are organised in the most helpful and efficient manner. Most would agree that regular testing of some sort is essential in order to assess how well students have learnt the curriculum. The National Curriculum has used the idea of standard assessment tasks (SATs) to achieve this aim. SATs are to be taken by all pupils at ages 7, 11, and 14. Much debate has focused on this aspect of the curriculum, and the issues involved have been extremely complex.

Changes in testing
The National Curriculum has involved some changes in the way schools and teachers will use test marks and grades, and these need a little explanation.

The tests involved in the National Curriculum do not involve ranking your child against other children either in the same class or school, or indeed nationally.

Ranking, a common way of looking at ability, is in truth not very helpful. Your child could be in the middle of a class of very able students, or top of a weak group, for instance. Such relative descriptions tell us little about your child's real ability, and only encourage them to feel unjustifiably elated or depressed.

What parents and students really need is some more objective measure of the student's achievements - in other words we need to know what is a very good, a good, and a weak performance in any particular subject.

What will the SATs tell me?

The aim of the SATs are to provide an accurate demonstration of what the pupil has achieved. Each subject area is broken down into various levels of attainment - most subjects have 10 levels up to KS3, and each level can be described in terms of various (usually a large number!) of attainment targets. You do not really need to worry too much about the fine detail of all this. What you do need as a parent is to understand the overall structure. This will enable you to ask your child's teachers the relevant questions on parents' evenings etc. For instance, you may wish to ask what level of attainment your child has achieved and whether this is true of their overall performance in the subject, or just for a few aspects of the subject. In English, for example, your child may have reached a high level for oral work, but could be lagging a little in written work, or in spelling. These areas of strength and weakness are not necessarily anything to worry too much about. Most people will have areas of strength and weakness in any task they carry out, but you will want to know what the areas are and what can be done about the weaknesses.

Open enrolment

One of the most important changes in the ways schools are run has been the decision to allow open enrolment. Prior to the 1988 Education Reform Act, schools usually enrolled students on the basis of whether they lived in the school 'catchment area'.

Now parents can apply to any school to admit their child, and this is referred to as open enrolment.

In theory you are free to apply to any school you wish - it no longer has to be the school closest to your home.

Will I be able to send my child to any school?
This sounds ideal, but of course there are some strings attached. The only grounds which a school may give for refusal of admission is that it has no spare places, in other words, that it is full. There are government regulations which define what 'full' means for any particular type of school. This is done either by means of a historical comparison (how many pupils the school had in 1980), or based on a formula.

What this means for parents is that although in theory you have a completely free choice, in practice constraints will be put on your choice. Some schools will inevitably become more popular than others, and in these schools there will be competition for places. How schools cope with this competition will vary.

- Research local schools.
- Decide which ones appeal to you.
- Find out what their admissions policies are.

In many cases residence close to the school still counts, but this can be especially complex if you live close to a county or LEA boundary, even though schools are no longer run by the LEAs!

In some cases your child may stand a better chance if they have a brother or sister at the school, or if the school is 'voluntary aided' by a church, you may find that it will help if you are a practising member of that church. However, in this last case, church schools will often admit children of other faiths - rules vary.

How to appeal

There are no simple solutions to getting your child into your first choice school. To maximise your chances, it is vital you research schools' admissions policies. If your application is refused, you can appeal.

In the first instance you would ask the school to initiate appeal proceedings, but if this failed and you were not satisfied with the reasons given, you would have the option to appeal to the Local Government Ombudsman (see Help List).

Again, if this stage were to be unsuccessful, you could appeal to the Secretary of State for Education, and take the matter up with your MP.

Opting out

Another of the changes in the education system has been the opportunity for schools to opt out of local authority control (see also Chapter 1). Opted out schools are called Grant Maintained (GM) schools. These schools are funded directly by central government, instead of receiving funds from, and being managed by, the local authority. This means that the school has to undertake all its own management and administration, ordering of supplies, staff recruitment and training, and so on.

The new government guidelines state that all parents should have the right to vote whether they wish their child's school to become a GM school. Parents can insist that the school governors hold a ballot to determine whether a majority of parents wish the school to become Grant Maintained. However, in many cases the decision to apply for GM status will be initiated by the Governors and Headteacher, although they have to show that a majority of parents want this.

In addition, school governing bodies have to consider whether a ballot of parents on GM status should be held every year, and they must report and explain the decision in their annual report to parents.

1988 Education Reform Act - Summary

- Education to be organised around 4 Key Stages.
- Standard Assessment Tasks at 7, 11, and 14.
- Core and Foundation subjects.
- Open Enrolment.
- Opting out of LEA control - Grant Maintained Status.

So why opt out?

Those who support the idea of opting out argue that it will give schools more freedom to organise and manage the school in ways which the senior staff and governors see fit.

This would include financial decisions, so that a GM school could for instance decide that funds could be spent on a new minibus, rather than on textbooks.

In addition though, schools which have opted out have gained extra funding.

Other reasons for opting out could be when a local authority wants to change the character of the school. They may for instance, want to make it a mixed school. In this case, going GM could be a good solution.

Are there any disadvantages with GM status?

There could be various disadvantages with GM status. Schools have gained many advantages from local authority control, including staff recruitment and training, the educational psychologist service, Special Needs advice and services, catering, library services, building and maintenance services.

Once a school has left the control of a local authority, all of these services will have to be paid for out of the school's own funds.

There is a very real danger that costs for GM schools will increase, and they will find themselves in a much more competitive and unprotected environment.

Summing up...

It should be pretty clear that schools and education have changed a lot since most parents were at school. You should now have a good idea how schools are organised and what they are teaching nowadays. We now need to think about how to choose the right school for your child.

3 HOW TO CHOOSE AND GET INTO A GOOD SCHOOL

- What is good education?
- What is best for your child?
- Visiting schools
- Weighing it all up
- Beware of statistics
- Summing up...

Choosing a school is often a nerve-racking process for parents. It is easy to be put off a school because of some casual remarks made by others, or because of one's own impressions and prejudices.

You need to do your own research to get the real picture of what your local schools are like.

Try to talk to other parents, teachers, and don't forget the pupils themselves!

You should be able to find other parents willing to talk to you - you may know some personally, but if not, try contacting the PTA representatives.

The staff should certainly be willing to talk to you, and there may even be open evenings or days for prospective parents. Be sure to make use of these, as they are an invaluable opportunity to get into a school and ask questions about the things which most concern you.

Looking at a school and talking to staff and students is the best way to get a feel for the sort of place it is and the sort of education it offers.

How can I find out what a school is really like?
Talking to the students is an often neglected tactic, but it's an ideal way to find out what the school is really like. The students will experience far more lessons than anyone else (even school inspectors) and in a way they are the most important judges of a school.

Deciding which schools to apply to for admission, you will need to carefully weigh up what sort of student your child is, and what sort of school will best suit their needs. But what is good education?

What is good education?

There has been considerable debate in Britain about just what good education is. The media and others have sometimes exaggerated and simplified this debate as being one between 'progressives' and 'traditionalists'.

In this debate, progressives are generally shown as

believing in group work, giving children too much freedom and choice, and as being lax on discipline.

The so-called 'traditionalists', on the other hand, are portrayed as believing in the importance of the three R's (reading, writing, and arithmetic), learning factual knowledge by heart (sometimes called rote learning), and whole-class teaching.

Obviously, you will have your own views and preferences on this issue, and will want to choose a school which you feel reflects your views. You will find teachers who could be described by either of these terms in primary and secondary schools throughout the country.

You will also find many teachers who use ideas from a variety of sources, who would be difficult to categorise simply as either 'progressive' or 'traditionalist'.

So what are the best teaching methods?

Many educationists agree that good education involves a variety of teaching methods, and that the best teachers combine a mixture of the old and the new. Lack of discipline does not help anyone. But equally, rote learning alone does not help pupils understand the ideas they are being taught. And unless they can do this, they cannot use their memorised knowledge, however vast.

Good education then, is teaching and learning which involves a variety of methods, enabling pupils to acquire a wide range of skills.

It should also involve a broad and balanced range of subjects.

The three R's are no longer sufficient in a society which is changing rapidly.

Children and adults will need to know more, and to be adaptable and able to acquire new skills.

What is best for your child?

In a very real way, good education is the methods of teaching and the type of school which will best meet the needs of your child. If your child doesn't enjoy traditional academic subjects then they will no doubt be better off in a school which doesn't put too much stress on academic success.

This doesn't mean that such a school is a bad school: it might for instance provide excellent vocational education, or perhaps emphasise arts and creative skills. If your child works better in a less formal situation, they may well respond better in a school which has few formal regulations - with no school uniform, for instance.

Of course, this doesn't mean that you allow your child to make bad decisions and convince you to help them choose a school for the wrong reasons. People - young and old, are adept at deceiving themselves and resistant to unpleasant truths.

How can I help my child choose the right school?

It is your job as a parent to try to understand and know your child. The better you can do this, the more you will be able to help them gain self-knowledge. This is the key ingredient for a successful education.

Make sure that you discuss with your child what their strengths and weaknesses are, and what direction their interests lie in. Both of you can then come to a more informed decision about what it is you want from education.

Visiting schools

Once you have decided what sort of school will best suit your child's needs, and researched your local schools' enrolment policies, you are in a position to start further research. Hopefully, this stage of the process will involve you in visiting schools and looking around. If your local schools do not offer this opportunity, through an open evening for instance, invite yourself. Don't feel too embarrassed to phone up and ask if you can visit.

What to look for and what to ask

Once you get into a school you have a good opportunity to judge the quality of education it provides. It can be good to see the school during a normal teaching day, although obviously this may be difficult to arrange, but you should at least be able to talk to staff and students.

What makes a good learning environment?
A good classroom will have displays (even in secondary schools) on the wall, hopefully including students' work. You will want to make sure that the environment is stimulating and cheerful. Ask yourself whether you would like to sit in the classroom several times a week.

What else should I look for?
There are usually a number of clues within classrooms as to how children are taught, and indeed things which can indicate how lively a school is.

Are the desks arranged in rows, or are they grouped or in a horseshoe pattern around the room?

Rows would indicate a more traditional type of teaching, groups a more modern and active style.

A horseshoe configuration may be used more frequently in the sixth form, and allows for discussion work centred around the teacher, who acts as a chairperson.

Of course you have to be careful in interpreting this sort of evidence! Teachers may well come in and change all the furniture around before starting their lesson.

Other things to look out for

There are other clues to be on the look out for. We have already mentioned displays of work, but it is worth thinking about this a little more.

- Try to see if the work is recent.
- Is there work on display throughout the school, or is it just in some rooms?
- You could ask whether it has been done by one class, or comes from several classes.
- What you are trying to find out is whether the displays are typical or just one-off things which are done to impress parents. Equally noticeboards are valuable clues to the level of activity going on in the school. Does there seem to be a lot of information displayed? Do there appear to be lots of different activities being organised?

Physical environment

You will also be able to size up the school in terms of its general cleanliness, absence or otherwise of graffiti, and so on. If there is temporary accommodation such as portacabins, do take a look at it to see that although temporary, it is made as comfortable as possible. You could try to find out whether use of such facilities is shared around to ease the discomfort.

What sort of questions should I ask staff?

In addition to all this, you will need to ask the staff and students questions. Here are a few examples on the sorts of issues that will probably concern you most:

Checklist - things to ask staff

- What are the GCSE pass rates like?
- Will I be charged for exam fees?
- How does the tutorial system work?
- How do you help new students settle in?
- Is there a bullying problem?
- Does the school have a policy to prevent bullying?
- How much homework do students in 1st/2nd year etc get?
- Is there a homework diary or system? (if no, why not?)
- How are lates/absences checked?
- What do I do if my child is absent?
- What is staff absence like?
- How many times will my child's lessons be covered by a teacher other than one who is timetabled to teach them?

Checklist - things to ask pupils

- What are the lessons like?
- Do you enjoy the school?
- What is the best thing about the school?
- Do you get regular homework?
- What happens if you don't do your homework?
- What happens if someone misbehaves in a lesson?
- Do students generally behave well?
- What's your favourite lesson and why?

Weighing it all up

Of course, you need to be critical in your assessment of the answers you get to these questions. Is there any other evidence to back up the claims made by staff and students? Schools are now required by the government to produce examination and results of SATs, and an annual report to be made available to parents. You do need to examine this material carefully, since schools obviously want to show themselves in the best possible light.

How to interpret school publicity

As mentioned, schools are now legally obliged to provide comprehensive information on their exam results, and this in combination with the increasing competition for pupils, has meant that more and more schools are producing glossy brochures aimed at showing off their wares to parents. As with all glossy brochures, be aware that they might not always give the whole picture.

What should the prospectus tell me?

- School prospectuses should give you comprehensive information about what is taught throughout the school.
- It should inform you of the school's tutorial and pastoral systems, and give a clear indication of any further academic and pastoral support available.
- It should also provide basic information regarding school terms, attendance and notification of absence policies, and if relevant, details of school uniform.

The school is obliged to publish its exam results for GCSE and A level and the results of any SATs taken by pupils. These results do not, strictly speaking, have to appear in the prospectus, but they are often included.

Should I believe everything I'm told?

There are several points to be wary of when looking at school publicity. Firstly, beware of glossy pictures showing gleaming equipment. These are a good starting point, but you should make sure that they represent facilities which are open to and used by all the students. The best science equipment or laboratory or language lab shouldn't be kept for a few small A level sets, for instance. Likewise, are the showpiece sports facilities reserved for the use of the school team only?

Beware of statistics

Remember that all GCSE grades down to G are strictly speaking passes, as are all A level grades between A and E. A school can quite legitimately say that it has a 100% pass rate at A level if all students entered for a subject gain at least an E grade. However, you may feel that looking at the number of grades between A and C is most appropriate for A levels.

In the case of GCSE's you can argue that it is even more important to indicate how many students achieved grades between A (or A*) and C.

Is there anything schools can do to improve their image?

Schools can 'adjust' their percentage of pass grades in other ways. They may withdraw the exam entries of students whom they feel will perform poorly. Perhaps few teachers would support such action, but it can happen. Sometimes withdrawing a student's entry can be the student's own fault, say through persistent absence or failure to complete work. In these sorts of cases schools and colleges may refuse to pay the student's examination fees, and the student is said to be an 'unsupported' candidate, ie the school does not support the entry and does not pay the exam fee.

What counts as a pass?

These types of practice can lead to a lot of 'editing' of examination statistics. If teachers or schools tell you that their pass rate is for example, 90%, ask them to explain what that figure includes, what they count as a pass, how many students they entered, and how it compares with previous years and other schools.

How to interpret school league tables

League tables are another aspect of the new education system we now have to grapple with. Many of the same sorts of criticism and cautions made above can be applied to the league tables.

There have been many criticisms made of league tables, and not just from teachers and educationists. League tables can be very appealing, for they seem to make it clear which schools are performing and which are failing. However, there is a very good case for suggesting that things aren't quite as simple as this.

Problems with league tables

The league tables, as produced by the government, leave out some vital information and do not give a complete picture of what goes on in schools.

They do not tell us the ability level of students when they entered a school. In other words they don't tell us much about the quality of the 'raw materials' which the teachers had to work with.

A school could be doing an excellent job getting grade D GCSE passes out of some students - perhaps another school would only have managed an E grade. Nevertheless, in the league tables, both simply appear as low grades, not worthy of any particular praise. Additionally, a school's performance in exams can vary quite a lot from year to year, simply because the standard of the students varies.

So finally...

In summary then, treat information about a school from the league table cautiously. Just because a school is not right up at the top, it does not follow that it is a poor school.

Debate about league tables will undoubtedly continue. Although many will criticise them, they are probably here to stay, and in a way, it is very hard to argue against them, since this sounds a bit like suggesting that the information about school performance must be kept secret. It could be suggested that in the long run, the publication of statistics on school performance will be a good thing, as long as it promotes debate about how the statistics are best interpreted.

Summing up...

To ensure that you are getting the best for your child, you need first of all to know and understand what best suits your child's needs.

Listen to your child. There is no single type of education or school which is right for everybody.

You also need to be confident in researching your local schools, and make sure that you ask them for as much help as you want.

Research carefully, ask the key questions, and ask awkward questions.

If you can do this, then you will already be doing a lot to help your child learn.

4 HOW TO HELP YOUR CHILD LEARN

- Avoiding pressure
- What can I do to help my child?
- Reading
- Writing
- Vocabulary
- Numeracy
- Homework
- What about GCSE or A Level coursework?
- Summing up...

Avoiding pressure

It's very easy to become a nagging parent. We frequently hear how parents may try to encourage their children to work hard at school by offering tempting rewards such as holidays, money, and so on. Teachers are often asked to help parents impose a hard-line disciplinary policy on children. You'll hear parents say things like, 'If he doesn't do his homework properly, keep him in detention, or tell him he won't play football.'

How would *you* feel?

Try to imagine how you would feel if you were treated like this at work. You might well become aggressive and uncooperative. If it was possible, you might leave and find employment elsewhere.

On the other hand, you might feel intimidated by the pressure put on you, and decide to keep your head down and avoid trouble. No one would notice that anything much had changed. The boss might think that all the trouble had blown over. All would be well, unless an inspection or a complaint from a vigilant customer drew unwanted attention to your work.

All these reactions can occur with school children who are pressurised, or threatened with some sort of punishment if their performance does not improve.

A way forward

All good teachers will tell you that one of the key skills required in teaching is that of encouraging and helping children to reach their potential, and yet at the same time, avoiding putting undue pressure on them. As a parent this is a skill which you, too, need to develop.

What can I do to help my child?

Listen to your child

One of the most important ways to avoid pressurising your child is to listen. If you are to help your child you need to know what they find difficult, what their strengths and their weaknesses are. You also have to learn to know your child and to accept them for what they are. If your child loves sport for instance, it is pointless to try and force them to become musical.

The American psychologist Howard Gardner has recently argued that rather than seeing intelligence as narrowly defined as being 'academic', we should recognise a variety of intelligences. Gardner talks about physical intelligence (sports), musical intelligence, scientific, artistic, linguistic, manual/practical, and other types of intelligence.

Encourage your child to experiment

Perhaps the point we should take from all this is that the best thing parents can do is to encourage their children to find out what they are good at. Usually we are successful in activities which we enjoy.

Of course, as a parent, you will need to encourage your child to work at all subjects or topics which they study, not just the ones which they are best at, but this has to be done sensitively. Let's look at how you can give your child this encouragement in all areas of learning.

Providing a stimulating environment

Perhaps the best thing you can do to help your child succeed educationally, is to give them a stimulating home environment.

What can I do at home to help my child learn?
You need to do all that you can to encourage your child to take an interest in the world they live in, to find out what skills they have and develop them, and to have lots of opportunities to gain new experiences.

In practice this means that you need to encourage them in hobbies, sports, musical and artistic activities.

You will need to provide your child with reading material as well as the latest videos and CD's.

You will need to make sure that you have some magazines, newspapers, and books in the home.

Make sure that you take your child on outings - to sports or cultural events, films or theatre, walks in the country, or whatever.

Encourage discussion
Try and make sure that your home environment is one where discussion and asking questions is encouraged, and where the parent is not automatically right. This will encourage your child to be enquiring.

Reading

When your child is very young, reading stories with them is one easy way to encourage them to develop their reading skills and imagination. It is very important, though, to ask your child lots of questions about the story. Ask them to explain:

- What is happening in the story
- Which characters they like
- Why they like them
- What they think will happen next

With young children who are starting to read, it's a good idea to have a regular time when you sit together and read. As they become more proficient readers they can do more and more of the reading. Once your child becomes a good reader, try to maintain the reading time. You can then remember to keep talking to them about what they have read. If your child finds reading a chore, the way to make it fun and engage their interest is to let them read about something that interests them.

It really doesn't matter if they are reading about football, pop stars, or whatever. The key thing is to get them reading. But do make sure that the reading material varies and that your child doesn't just read the easiest available material.

You may have to search around and find books and magazines that will gently stretch your child. Given the huge range of books available for children nowadays, this shouldn't be too difficult. If in doubt consult your local bookshop.

'...oh yes, I remember this one...
could I read it to you before bedtime, dad?'

Writing

Encouraging your child to write in the early stages of developing writing skills can follow similar lines. Try to make writing a game. Your child could for instance practice the alphabet by making pictures to illustrate letters.

As your child becomes older there are all sorts of activities which can be done. Encourage your child to keep a scrapbook. Once again, it doesn't matter too much what they put in a scrapbook, it might be about football, pop music, or television.

Other ideas

You could also persuade your child to write the shopping list each week, or perhaps to make you a list of the times of your essential television viewing (copied out of the newspaper). As your child becomes more proficient you could encourage them to keep a diary, either throughout the year, or perhaps just for special occasions, such as holidays.

The diary in turn can become something which you can talk about together. Holiday postcards and thank-you letters are of course further opportunities to make sure that your child gets more practice with writing - insist that they write them!

Vocabulary

A good vocabulary is essential for educational success.

Encouraging and helping your child to read and write will of course help them to develop a good vocabulary. In addition, it can be a good idea to find activities which will specifically help to improve your child's vocabulary. Here are a few ideas:

- There are many word games available in toyshops and bookshops and these are well worth sifting through.
- There are also many crossword and word puzzle books available.
- Many children love making up their own crosswords or word hunt games (word squares) and these can be an ideal solution for wet weather or long car journeys.

Give them a dictionary and let them get on with it!

Numeracy

Even if you were never particularly confident with numbers yourself, you can still do a lot to help your child with basic numeracy skills.

When should I start?
It's a good idea to get your child used to numbers well before school. Simple counting games are quite sufficient to help develop confidence with numbers and provide a good foundation once your child reaches primary school. Just counting the stairs as you walk up or down them, or counting cutlery and plates after washing up, will help your child learn numbers. You may even see conscientious parents getting their children to count potatoes or onions into a bag at the supermarket!

Later on when your child starts primary school, you may want to ensure that your child learns multiplication tables. Teachers point out, rightly, that learning tables is in itself not enough to ensure your child develops a strong understanding of numbers. But many agree that it helps considerably. You can help your child by getting them to practice their tables. There are several videos and audiotapes available, which try to put the multiplication tables to music - with varying degrees of success!

Homework

Once children start secondary school, it is usually a requirement that they complete formal homework tasks.

Can I help with homework?

It is perfectly acceptable for parents to help their children with homework, although we do have to be clear about what we mean by help - it does not mean that parents do the homework. Certainly parents need to make sure that their children do the required homework. Some things which you could do, are:

- Try to take an interest in your child's work, and ask them what they are working on, whether it is easy, difficult, enjoyable and so on.
- You may want to help by, for instance, suggesting that your child writes an essay plan.
- You can then check the essay plan, and maybe suggest alterations.
- You can check the final draft, for example for spelling mistakes.

What about GCSE or A Level coursework?

If your child is doing GCSE or A Level coursework, the issue of help becomes more complex. Your child must sign a document to ensure that the work is their own. If you follow the advice on the previous page, there should be no question that the work is your child's and not yours. Your child will, though, have had what may in effect be an extra lesson. This may mean that children whose parents have had a high level of education will be advantaged. What do you do if you don't fit into this category? There are some ways around this.

If you are really determined, there is nothing to stop you enrolling at a local evening class to follow the same course as your child, and thus give them help. But you can't do this for every subject your child is studying. This book provides a variety of suggestions. Think through your options and circumstances carefully before deciding your own best course of action.

How much time should be spent on homework?
The time requirements of homework can vary greatly, depending on the abilities of the child, courses being studied and other factors. A rough guide might be to suggest that children starting secondary school in year 7 would do about half an hour per evening, increasing by about a quarter of an hour each year, so that by year 11 (GCSE year) students would be averaging one and a half hours per evening (these would be a suggested minimum).

The key thing is to make sure that your child completes homework regularly for all subjects being studied, and develops good study techniques.

Homework requires a quiet space to work away from distractions, and with books and other necessary equipment easily to hand.

A Level students

A level students should be spending about five hours per subject per week on homework. Some may well spend more than this. A levels require a lot of reading and/or problem solving, and this is why the time requirement increases so much.

How to help checklist

- Listen to your child
- Find out your child's strengths and weaknesses
- Make time for regular discussion
- Read regularly with your child
- Use number/word/writing games to encourage your child
- Provide a stimulating environment

Summing up...

You don't have to be an expert to help your child learn. You do have to work hard to listen to your child, and take an interest in what they do, without being pushy. Give your child lots of space, and lots of activity. Encourage them to take a questioning attitude to life. Be their friend and always encourage them to have a go. Give them confidence, and you'll be amazed at what they can achieve.

5 HOW TO KEEP IN TOUCH WITH THE SCHOOL

- Your rights and responsibilities
- How to deal with teachers
- When problems arise
- Contacting the school
- How to deal with the authorities
- PTA's
- Governors
- Summing up...

Once you have found a place for your child in a school that you and your child are happy with, it is important to remember that your work is not over. You will need to keep in touch with the school in order to ensure that your child is making progress. This is not always an easy thing to do, but this chapter will show you what to expect and how to make sure that you get the help you need.

Your rights and responsibilities

The Parents' Charter, set up in 1992 by the Government, now sets out a range of rights which parents can expect from schools. The main rights in the Charter can be seen in the table below.

The Government's Parents' Charter points out a number of other rights which parents have, but this chapter will focus on your rights regarding the information you should receive from schools, and what you can do to improve communication between school and parents.

Parents charter

Parents have a right to:

- Receive a written report on their child's progress at least once a year.
- Receive regular reports from school inspectors.
- See performance tables (including exam results) for all local schools every year.
- Receive a prospectus or brochure about individual schools.
- Receive a prospectus (including exam results) every year.
- Receive an annual report from the school governors.

What information do schools have to provide?

In general what the recent legislation means is that schools have to provide parents with information on the following:

- Examination performance, absenteeism, progress of students.
- The first destinations of pupils leaving the school, the school budget.
- The results of school inspections.
- Who parents should contact to discuss their child's progress.

- Your responsibilities are basically to ensure that your child attends school regularly.

How to keep in touch with the school

In building up a relationship with your child's school, you need to take the initiative to make sure the school knows your views. However, you need to do this carefully, and avoid becoming a nuisance. The most important issue here is to build positive and constructive relationships with the people who teach your child.

How to deal with teachers

You will meet many types of teachers. Some may seem jaded, even cynical, whilst others will seem thoroughly professional and objective in judging the achievements of your child. Most will probably lie somewhere between these two extremes. Teachers can be working under considerable stress. This can make them defensive, as can criticism in general.

The important point here for parents, is not to expect teachers to be superhuman. Teachers do not know everything - either about the subject they teach, or life in general. It is important to see yourself and your child's teachers as equal partners in your child's education.

Meeting your child's teachers

When you meet your child's teachers it may be helpful to ask if there is anything that you can do to help your child's progress. Equally though, it is the teacher's job to teach, and you will want to know that this is being done satisfactorily. You can assess this by asking whether your child participates well in lessons, whether they are completing homework on time, and how they can improve.

What sort of questions should I ask teachers?

You may want to ask the teacher to give some indication of how they teach. Teachers should be prepared to tell parents about their teaching methods, without going into lengthy theoretical explanations. You might find it helpful to ask the teacher what sort of activities they typically do in a lesson, and what they do to help children who find the work either hard or easy.

What to look for

Hopefully teachers will be able to demonstrate that they use a range of activities which fully involve children of all abilities, avoiding making the work too difficult or too easy. This would be teaching to the 'middle' ability children in the group. The problem with it is that it doesn't stretch the most able, and leaves the least able stranded. These points are applicable to any teaching group, because even if they have been streamed in some way, there will still be differences in their abilities.

You may also want to ensure that teachers work in a

systematic way and cover all the items in the National Curriculum, or in the exam syllabus your child is studying. In this case, it might be useful to ask the teacher if you can see their 'scheme of work'. The scheme of work is simply an outline plan of what the teacher will be teaching over a term or year, and gives brief details of the topics to be taught and the methods to be used.

A good school will encourage you to contact teachers by telephone if you have any concerns, and should matters require it, invite you in for further discussion with staff.

When problems arise

Problems can arise at any time in your child's education, and it's safe to say that every student and every parent will have problems of some kind. The more knowledgeable you are about the education system, and the more time you have spent talking to school, teachers, and your child, the better you will be able to deal with the problems when they arise.

Problems may be of various types. It may be that your child is not performing well at school. It may be that you are unhappy with something which the school is doing. There may be problems of bullying or discipline, where your child may be the victim or the perpetrator of unwanted behaviour.

What should I do if a problem arises?
Firstly, remember that the problem may not be result of the school and the teachers. It might be the case that your child has been misbehaving. If this is so, then you will have to help your child to face up to their responsibilities. Teachers and schools, no matter how good, cannot achieve miracles. Learning is a cooperative endeavour.

Contacting the school

Whatever the particular circumstances, try not to let off steam at teachers and the school, no matter how annoyed you feel. You may lose credibility and your child may suffer as a result. Try to contact the school immediately so that you can register your concern - if you delay doing this it can weaken your case, perhaps because it implies a lack of urgency.

Who should I contact?
Usually the most appropriate person to contact is your child's form tutor. However, it may be appropriate in some cases to approach either a particular subject teacher, or if you feel it is a very serious matter, then the Headteacher or Deputy Head. The school prospectus should make clear whom to contact in case of enquiries.

What if I don't like talking to people in authority?
If you are unconfident in dealing with the school, it's a

good idea to get a friend or adviser to come with you in any discussions with the school staff. Good examples of people who may be able to help you would be, a solicitor, social worker, friend, or PTA representative.

Whatever your problem, you will be able to appeal against most decisions made by the school - including decisions to exclude or suspend a student, special educational needs provision, and decisions not to give your child a place in a school.

Perhaps the most important advice to bear in mind when problems arise though, is to keep lines of communication with the school open. This is vital if you are to effectively monitor and help your child's progress through the school.

How to deal with the authorities

The term 'authorities' here refers to the larger bureaucracies governing the education service. The main authorities a parent might typically deal with would be, the Local Education Authority, and perhaps Examination board.

Dealing with bureaucracies is rarely going to be an enjoyable activity, and indeed it can be a rather intimidating process for the individual trying to (frequently) battle against a large organisation.

What sort of issues lead to disputes?

You may have some contact with authorities when applying to schools, or if there are problems over your child's attendance. The authorities also step in when exclusions, suspensions, and grants are concerned. Examination boards are another form of authority you may have to deal with should you decide to appeal for a remarking of your child's examination script.

Your rights and responsibilities - what to do

- You should spend some time making sure that you understand what your rights are, and then be persistent, but polite, in trying to pursue them.
- If you have difficulty with the authorities over your child's attendance, or over a decision to exclude, you may have some mitigating circumstances.
- If this is the case you need to inform the school as soon as possible.
- If you are worried that your child might truant, you need to raise the matter before problems arise.

Remember, your responsibility is to ensure that your child attends school.

You can get further information on most of these sorts of issues from the Citizens Advice Bureau, your child's school, and the DFEE who produce a wide range of helpful leaflets (see Help List).

Keeping in touch - checklist

- Read the Parents' Charter
- Obtain and read copies of the school's prospectus and annual reports
- Make sure that you receive and read your child's reports
- Consider joining the PTA
- If problems arise, consult with school staff promptly, and take further advice if necessary (see Help List for useful addresses)
- Should you have to meet school staff, take a friend or a professional who can act as an advisor

If disputes do arise with the school, keep copies of all letters between yourself and the school, and make notes of any telephone conversations you have.

PTA's

Parent Teacher Associations are an important way for parents to take a greater role in the running of schools. They are also a good way for you to get to know the staff and learn more about how the school works. If your child's school doesn't have a PTA contact the Headteacher and suggest that one is started.

What do PTA's do?

PTA's undertake a variety of activities such as fund raising, campaigning, and providing voluntary help with school activities. If you have special skills, for example you are a builder or a solicitor, you may be able to help the school with informal advice. You can help in some way whoever you are. Why not get involved, in however small a way?

Governors

School governors play an important role in the running of a school, and they are also a vital means of maintaining and developing contact between parents and school. School governing bodies are required to have several parent governors. You will have a right to vote for parent governors who can represent the views of parents on the governing body.

Any parent with a child at the school can stand for election as a parent governor. If you don't want to be a parent governor yourself, it's a good idea to find out who the parent governor is, so that you can contact them if necessary.

What do Governors do?

Governors now have several duties which are particularly worth mentioning here.

The governing body of a school has to produce an annual report which must be sent to all parents. This will give details of exam results, absenteeism rates, as well as details of the school budget. The budget is worth looking at to check that your school is spending its money effectively.

The annual report will also have to show that the issue of GM status has been considered, as discussed previously.

The governors are required to arrange an annual meeting which is open to parents, giving an opportunity for more detailed questioning and discussion.

If the school has recently been inspected then the governors must provide a summary of the inspection report to parents, together with the governing bodies response to the report and plans on how to best develop the school.

At the annual meeting the governing body would be expected to demonstrate what they have done to implement any changes required as a result of inspection.

Summing up...

Keeping in touch with your child's school can be done in several ways: through your own contact with teachers; through the information schools are now required by law to provide; through playing a role with the PTA and Board of Governors. Of course you will need to do much to monitor your child's progress. The next chapter will examine how we can do this, and what we need to look for.

6 HOW TO CHECK YOUR CHILD'S PROGRESS

- Is your child making progress?
- What should I look for in a good report?
- What can I do to help my child?
- What counts as progress?
- Continuous improvement
- Homework policies
- Records of achievement (ROA's)
- Options at 14 and 16
- Summing up...

Is your child making progress?

Most parents are very concerned to find out whether their child is making progress in their school work. There are a number of ways in which you can gain a good idea of how your child is progressing.

Firstly, you will need to try and ensure that you get feedback from both your child and the school. Feedback from your child may be in the form of comments during the term; comments from the school will generally be a formal written report. The feedback you gain from your child will depend on your relationship with your child. If you can examine your child's work without this being seen as undue pressure or nagging, you can probably assess their capabilities and progress.

If you have followed the advice in this book, the chances are that both you and your child will enjoy discussing school work, and that your child will actually ask for help if in difficulty.

Your other source of information will be the school report.

What should I look for in a good report?

If your child is to make progress, it is vital that school reports are accurate and give a clear indication of your child's current abilities and achievements, as well as what they should do to improve.

Even if a child is performing to a very high standard, a report should be able to suggest how the student might be stretched still further, in order to achieve the best that they are capable of.

Teachers comments in reports have sometimes been cryptic and unhelpful. The 'could do better' type of comment have passed into folklore. You should look out for the following:

- Reports should not be sarcastic, and should attempt to give an objective comment on the work done and the standards achieved.

- A good report should also give details of attendance, and any test or examination results.
- A good report which does these things will enable you and your child to see what needs to be done, eg comments such as, 'needs to do more reading', 'must take more care over writing up experiments', 'spelling needs attention'.
- If the report doesn't achieve these things, then it is not a good or a very helpful report and you may want to take the matter up with the school.

Computerised reports

There are now several computer packages available which will produce school reports. These packages vary, from those which are basically specialised word processing packages, to those which will produce 'tailor-made' comments. There are various approaches to such packages.

Some would say that they are impersonal and inaccurate, whilst others may see them as a perfectly legitimate labour saving device. You will have to come to your own decision, but it may be worth asking teachers whether any such packages are used in the school. Bear in mind that most schools will be using computer packages of some sort, given growing information needs and demands on teachers' time.

What should I do if I am unhappy with a report?

You may be dissatisfied with a report about your child. You might see it as unfair, or not offering enough helpful advice, for instance. If this applies to only one subject, then it would probably be best to take the issue up with the subject teacher.

If you feel more strongly about the issue, or if it involves performance in several subjects, then it may be more useful to raise it with the form tutor, and maybe Head of Year. You also need to remember to avoid seeming aggressive. It's also worth bearing in mind that a problem may not have been caused by one teacher. It could be that there is a problem in the way the school reporting process is carried out.

Whatever problems you meet, remember that you need to try and work with the school. What you want is a helpful resolution of the problem which allows your child to make progress in their education.

Why is my child not making satisfactory progress?
You may feel that the school report has been compiled in a very professional manner, but nevertheless, you just do not feel that your child is making sufficient progress. In these sorts of cases you first need to make sure that the report is providing a clear indication of your child's progress.

You then need to check if your child is doing their best. If you, your child, and the teachers all agree a real effort is being made, you may wonder what more can be done. In such cases, it is as well to avoid pressurising your child, and important to remember that progress is often made gradually. Improvement by a student may often follow a long period of effort - maybe as much as several years.

What can I do to help my child?

However, there are some things which you can do to try and ensure that progress is more likely. Many schools will ask students to make an action plan in consultation with their teachers. The action plan can itemize in detail what the student needs to do, and build in regular reviews with a teacher.

Action plans

An action plan may help highlight a particular area of weakness.

- It may be that discussing an action plan highlights the need for other types of support, such as individual help etc.
- Extra help and more individual attention are often required by students who are not progressing as well as they could do.
- Some schools offer extra tuition in lunchtimes or after school.

If your child's school doesn't offer these sorts of help, you could suggest that it takes up some of the ideas mentioned.

Avoid pressurising

You need to be careful in emphasising the importance of academic progress to a child. If extra attention is seen as being either punitive or unduly pressuring, then it will probably be resented. You cannot force your child to make progress at a certain rate. The best way to ensure that your child makes adequate progress, is to encourage them in their efforts, which will make them keen to learn.

What counts as progress?

Some parents can tend to take the view that the way to measure their child's progress is by comparing the child to others in the school, or those in the same class. However tempting this may be, it is not the most helpful way of measuring progress. In the long run, it is better to compare a child against their own previous achievements.

The reason for this is that for some children, to compare them against the high flyers will be so demoralising that they may give up. Psychological and educational research tells us that people who are encouraged will have a greater sense of self-esteem and will be more likely to continue and improve their efforts.

Set realistic goals

A good example here is to think about how you could improve your own time for the hundred metres sprint. If you were continually having to train against or compare yourself to an Olympic athlete, you might well give up, feeling, perhaps realistically, that you would never match such a performance.

However, if you focused on your own performance, no matter how poor, you could gain satisfaction from reaching your own goals.

Continuous improvement

Along with this view goes the idea that you can always keep improving your performance. Alternatively, if a child reaches the point where it is felt, by either the child, the teachers, or parents, that a peak has been reached, it may be that there is some other area or skill which can be focused on. So in this sense, improvement is continuous.

As always, it is important to remember to avoid pressurising your child. Praise them for their efforts, even if they haven't improved a great deal, as long as they have tried hard.

Homework policies

Students need to do homework in order to make academic progress. All schools should therefore, have a common homework policy and teachers should be able to tell you how much homework is required in each year. Some schools require students to keep a homework diary.

Whatever method is used some system is needed to check that homework is done. If your child's school does not have such a system you should suggest it adopts one and makes sure that it is effective.

How important are mock exams?
All schools should hold mock exams for GCSE's and A levels, which should give an accurate indication of your child's progress and a predicted grade. You need to feel confident that the predicted grade your child receives is an honest one, since it does nobody any favours to get a false boost, only to be disappointed later.

However, if your child does perform badly in a mock exam, it is not the end of the world, since it can give a student a nasty reminder that they have not done sufficient revision, or point out an area of weakness. Appropriate action can then be taken.

Records of achievement - ROA's

Records of Achievement (ROAs or NRAs - National Records of Achievement) are a national initiative which started in the late 1980s. The aim of ROAs was to broaden the recording of students' achievements, and to recognise that achievement takes many forms. School is not just about exam passes: students can also achieve in sports and the arts, and they may make contributions to the school and wider community in many other ways.

What is the point of a Record of Achievement?
ROA's involve a yearly recording of the student's achievements. These are kept in a folder and can be presented to employers or colleges and universities. ROAs

also try to promote the idea that students have to take more responsibility for their own learning.

It is hoped that this can be achieved by requiring students to comment on what they feel their achievements are each year. Students are also encouraged to think about their future plans, and are required to make an action plan for each school year. This encourages students to start planning their own higher education and career goals.

ROA's and further education training
ROA's are especially important for students going on to further education, since they have to show FE colleges an action plan to gain admission for some courses. The action plan is also needed to gain funding for some courses from Training and Enterprise councils.

Why do ROA's matter?
ROA's are also important for A level/GNVQ students because the yearly personal statements give them practice for writing university entrance or job application forms. While universities and employers will still give weight to exam passes, an ROA is still beneficial for students. It can make them think about what they've been doing and where they want to go.

Options at 14 and 16

An important part of progress is working out what to do at key points in a young person's educational career. The choices at 14 are important because this will determine GCSE choices, which will in turn determine what A level or GNVQ options are most likely. Students should try to aim for breadth and balance of subjects, and not just choose the subjects they enjoy. This gives them the widest possible choice after GCSE.

Choices at 16

Choices at 16 require students to make choices which will take them towards certain career paths. For most the choice involves deciding whether to move towards the academic opportunities offered by an A level course, or taking a vocational course. Whatever course your child decides to take, numeracy and literacy, and nowadays computer literacy, are the key skills which they need to develop.

Try to ensure that these key skills will be included, whatever options your child takes. They are the key skills that employers will be seeking.

You need to ensure that your child makes the most of the advice of school and careers service, since the more specific a student can be about what they are interested in doing, the more helpful the advice can be.

Summing up...

Your child will make good progress if you can help them pace their efforts carefully. This often means letting them explore their own abilities gradually, but it doesn't mean a relaxed and carefree approach should be taken. You can help them to continually try to improve their work and make progress by focusing their attention on their own performance. Your child will not make progress if they are constantly looking over their own shoulder.

Checklist for progress

- Discuss work with school
- Discuss work with your child
- Encourage your child
- Don't compare them to other students
- Check advice given in reports
- Check any issues arising with school
- Check school homework policy
- Check whether extra help is necessary
- Discuss mock exam results with child and teachers
- Research GCSE and Post-16 courses

7 FINANCIAL AND LEGAL MATTERS

- Education for free?
- Post 16 Education
- Higher Education
- Getting help
- Health and safety
- Summing up...

Education for free?

In some senses your child can gain an excellent education from primary school all the way to postgraduate training for free. Of course, in another sense, even if you do make the most of your entitlements, you will probably have paid for these services through the tax system.

Nevertheless, while you can gain an excellent education without paying fees, there is increasing financial pressure on the education system, which means making some provision of your own is a sensible strategy.

What can I do to make things easier?

- Try to make some regular savings commitments specifically for your child's education. A building society account, Tessa, or Child Bonds, are all good options.
- You can use the money which you save to pay for 'extras', which might include school trips, equipment, extra private tuition. Or it could be useful to help finance your child through further education or university.
- Investigate the possible sources of grants and awards which may be open to you.

In addition to the general state benefits, such as higher education grants, there are a number of charitable awards and foundations for children or parents in particular circumstances. There are, for instance, charities for children of servicemen, clergymen, and so on.

Your local Citizens Advice Bureau or library can provide you with information and advice on relevant charities.

Post-16 education

After compulsary education, until the age of 19, your child is entitled to a free education. After the age of 19, they will be charged fees to study A Levels, GCSE's or GNVQ's. Often these fees are small, however, and many further education colleges and local education authorities will provide assistance.

Higher education

Students wishing to go on to higher education face a more complex situation. If a student gains a place in a UK university and is aged between 18 and 24, they will in most cases be eligible to apply for a local authority grant and a student loan. The tuition fees for university students are paid for by local education authorities.

The cost of living for students - just as for everyone else - has risen, and yet student grants have not increased greatly over the last few years. To meet the additional costs students are now able, and in fact expected, to apply for a student loan.

How much will my child get?
The maximum grant available to a student for living expenses currently stands at £1710 per annum (£2105 in London). In addition to this, students may borrow up to £1645 per annum (£2035 in London). The maximum living allowance which a student can gain therefore is £3355 per annum (£4140 in London).

Do all students get the same amount?
The amount a student will receive as grant for living expenses depends on their parents income. Any student with parents earning over £16050 will find that the parents are expected to make a contribution, and the grant awarded will be reduced.

When parental income reaches around £38000 per annum, students will receive very little from local authorities. Parents need to think ahead, particularly if they have several children who will be going to university, since the costs become increasingly burdensome.

Get in touch with your LEA as soon as possible
Lastly on this issue, make sure that you remember to contact your local education authority in the January before your child hopes to start university, so that you can get an application form. The local authority needs to know in good time, and it is possible that your child's university place could be put at risk if your grant application is not received by the deadline. Applications for grants and payment of university fees - which will affect you whether or not your child qualifies for a living expenses grant - are usually due around May.

Getting help

There are various sources of help available to hard-pressed parents.

If your child is between 16 and 18 and enrolled on a full time course in further education or sixth form, you may well receive help with transport costs from your local education authority. You need to check this with your local education authority, since the exact regulations depend very much on local circumstances.

Is there any other help available?

You will also find that most further education colleges will have what is called an 'access fund'. This is basically a fund for cases of hardship. You should try not to feel embarrassed about asking whether you could apply for a grant from this fund, since it is a routine piece of administration and many students benefit from it every year.

Access funds

The fund is often used to help students with financing college residential trips, essential books or equipment, and many other types of case. Most schools and sixth form colleges will have a similar sort of arrangement, and all schools and colleges will have a welfare officer, counsellor or tutor who can provide further information on this issue.

Students over 19

- If your child is over 19, it is possible to apply for help from the access fund in further education colleges.
- You can also seek help from your local benefits office and careers office.
- It is possible to apply for a career development loan for instance, or if your child is over 19 and studying part-time, is disabled, or a single-parent student, various benefits are available.
- If your child falls into any of these categories, you can also check with your local authority as to whether you can apply for a discretionary award.

- Discretionary awards are basically awards which the local authority can make to those it feels are deserving cases, but which it is not under any legal obligation to provide, such as for instance a higher education grant.

Grants are a complex business, so you need to make sure that you gather as much information as possible. Make sure that you contact some of the services mentioned below.

Financial advice and help - who can help?

- Your local education authority
- Your child's school or college - Welfare officer or tutor
- Your local DSS office
- Your local Careers Service office
- Your local Citizens Advice Bureau
- Your local Library - for information about educational grants and charities

Health and safety

In legal terms all students are the responsibility of the school and the teachers while on school premises, or when engaged on any school activities. In their professional role, teachers are said to act 'in loco parentis', that is, in the place of the parent.

'...now let's visit the science block - an excellent example of the level of safety I feel exists within the entire school...'

Teachers' responsibilities

Teachers must be able to show that they have acted in a way likely to safeguard the well-being of their students. Schools are bound to obey the health and safety regulations, ensuring that the school is a safe working environment for staff and students, and that there are adequate procedures for dealing with hazards and any emergencies which may arise.

School trips

All good schools will provide various opportunities for trips, from day trips to longer visits abroad. These are all educationally useful if properly organised. A week-long skiing trip for instance, would enable students to experience a foreign culture, develop their independence, and even practise their foreign language skills, among other things. An adventure training course would similarly develop self-confidence, encourage team work, and a host of other practical and personal skills.

Should I let my child go on school trips?

In recent years there have unfortunately been several tragic accidents involving students on school organised trips. Many parents would agree that some risk is inevitable in such situations. You can minimise this risk by making sure that you receive some essential information from the school. This should be provided as a matter of course, but the following checklist will give you an indication of the key things to ask questions about.

Checklist

- Will there be a sufficient number of staff (of both sexes) accompanying students?
- Are staff suitably qualified? Have they run similar trips before?
- Are other non-school staff involved, eg at adventure centres? Are they qualified, registered, and insured? Ask for details
- Make sure you can have a detailed itinery of the trip
- Make sure adequate insurance arrangements have been made
- Ask for a contact telephone number and address
- Ensure that you are informed of any changes in time of return
- Ask what rules students will be asked to keep on the trip

Summing up...

Finance is not necessarily a barrier to getting a good education for your child. There are many sources of financial support available from schools and colleges, as well as educational charities and government agencies. A few phone calls or letters should enable you to receive more detailed information.

It is wise to plan ahead if you can, and this will undoubtedly make life easier as your child works through the school system. In the case of legal aspects, make sure that you know and defend your rights. Where insurance and the safety of your child are concerned, do not hesitate to press schools for the information which you require.

8 GETTING EXTRA HELP

- What are Special Educational Needs (SENs)?
- How do I know whether my child has SENs?
- What is statementing?
- The consultation process
- Your rights
- Summing up...

Estimates suggest that about a fifth of all school pupils will have some sort of learning difficulty at some point in their school career. Parents know that all children will cause concern at some stage. However, parents of children with some sort of mental or physical disability will have especially stressful and painful circumstances to cope with.

This chapter will help you to find out about the provisions made for children with learning difficulties, how the system works, and what rights you have.

What are Special Educational Needs (SENs)?

The term Special Educational Needs (SENs) refers to any sort of learning difficulty which requires special help or some special educational provision. The definition of SENs includes a wide variety of problems and involves a wide range of solutions.

- SENs can include mental or physical disability, such as Downs syndrome
- Deafness and blindness
- Emotional and behavioural difficulties
- Children whose first language is not English
- Children who are experiencing difficulties learning basic skills in English or Mathematics.

These are only a few examples, and learning difficulties may arise for all sorts of reasons.

How do I know whether my child has SENs?

SENs frequently become apparent in the early years of a child's education. Regular medical and developmental checks should uncover any problems that your child has with hearing and vision, which could of course affect their ability to learn.

If you have any concerns about your child's hearing or vision you should obviously promptly contact your doctor. Medical checks should also uncover any other physical or mental problem. If any problems are uncovered before your child is of school age, then action can be taken at an early stage to plan the educational provision which your child will require.

It's not always easy to diagnose SENs

In other cases, it may not be so easy to establish whether your child has any SENs. There have of course, been some well publicised cases where a child has experienced learning difficulties for some time but where professionals have been unable to diagnose the cause of the problem.

This has happened for instance, in cases of dyslexia, and Asperer's syndrome. This tells us that it is not always easy to diagnose a learning difficulty, but thankfully such cases are fairly unusual.

Who should I ask?

As long as you ensure that you take a fairly close interest in what your child does at school and at home, you should be in a good position to spot any serious learning difficulty which your child may have. If you have any worries or concerns the first port of call must be your child's teacher. If you can discuss your concerns with the teacher, they will be able to investigate them in greater depth, and if necessary refer them for other professional opinions.

Remember though, just because your child has some difficulty learning, it doesn't necessarily mean that it is a serious difficulty. As mentioned previously, many children will have learning difficulties, and these can vary a lot in their seriousness. Many problems can be solved fairly quickly if you raise them with your child's teachers at an early stage. If you feel that you want a second opinion, you can contact a parents' group, voluntary society, or Citizens Advice Bureau for further help (see Help List).

What is Statementing?

If a child is considered to have SENs, the local education authority will have to produce a document, known as a 'Statement' which identifies what the child's learning difficulties are, and how the local education authority will cater for the child's particular needs.

How long does it take?
Statementing can be a complex process, but it is now governed by rules which emphasise the rights of parents and children, and strict time limits are set for the various stages. In all it should take about six months from a child being drawn to the attention of the authorities, to a statement document being issued.

What is the process and how is it started?
Statementing can be started either by a school, or by a parent. If you had concerns about your child, you could first ask the school to investigate your child's progress.

All schools should have a teacher with special responsibility for SENs, and they should be involved in reporting back to any parent who raised concerns.

You could go straight to the local education authority, but it would be wise to inform the school that you intended to do this.

What happens after a request for assessment is made?
Several stages may follow on from an initial request for assessment.

The school may agree that a child has SENs and may ask the local authority to make what is known as a Statutory Assessment. This is basically a thorough investigation into a child's educational background, and the local authority may invite the opinion of a variety of professionals, such as social workers, educational psychologists, and teachers.

The local authority will be required to provide you with the name of the person responsible for communicating with you. It is very important for you to keep in touch with this 'named officer', especially if you have any complaints or problems which you may want to inform the LEA of.

The consultation process

Local authorities must inform the parents or guardians of children they are considering 'statementing', and parents must give their consent to requests for Statutory Assessments within twenty nine days.

If it is decided that a child does not require a statement of SENs after the statutory assessment, then the LEA has to give an explanation of their decision. The decision as to whether to proceed with a statutory assessment must be made within six weeks.

If it is decided that a statement of SENs is necessary, then the LEA will have a period of three months in which to make enquiries and give a decision.

You can appeal against a decision not to undertake an assessment by contacting the 'named officer' provided by the LEA.

The statement

A completed statement will give details as to what the particular educational needs of a child are, what special help will be given, and which school the child will attend. It may also include details about transport. Obviously, these are all details which you may not agree with. For instance, it may be that an LEA does not agree that your child is dyslexic, or they may say that provision for your child can only be made in a special school, which may not be what you want for your child.

You can appeal to a SENs tribunal if you are unhappy with certain parts of a statement document. Your LEA or Citizens Advice Bureau can give you details on how to contact a SENs tribunal. However, remember that there are strict time limits for appeals, and if you miss these it is very hard to get the case reconsidered.

Your rights

Throughout the process of statementing you have a number of rights.

- Firstly, your child's school should provide details of its SENs policy and complaints procedure.
- The LEA should also provide clear details of the statementing procedure and should keep you informed at all times.
- During the process you may be asked to attend interviews, as may your child. You have the right to be accompanied by either a friend or a professional to meetings with the LEA or school.
- You can accompany your child to most meetings with educational psychologists or specialist teachers, though there may be occasions when you are asked to leave the room.
- You will be able to see the statement document before it is completed, and any written evidence submitted with it, and you will be invited to make comments.
- You should be able to respond or appeal at any stage in the process.

What will a statemented child be taught?
Your child will have the right to receive a broad and balanced curriculum, although Headteachers have the right to withdraw children from National Curriculum subjects for limited periods of time in special circumstances.

You do have the right to choose which school your child attends, although the authorities will have to be satisfied that the school will be suitable, that the child's presence will not adversely effect others, and that it will be an efficient use of the LEAs resources.

Gifted children

Especially gifted children are an often neglected aspect of SENs, but it can be argued that they too have special needs which are often neglected by the education system.

This can make schools particularly frustrating institutions for such children, whose abilities may be threatening to some teachers. Of course, we should be wary of applying the title of 'gifted' too freely. if you have good grounds to think that your child may be unusually gifted (rather than just 'bright'!) contact the National Association For Gifted Children (see Help List).

Your rights - checklist

Make sure that you:

- See the school's SENs policy
- Give your permission to statutory consent
- Are consulted and respond at all stages
- Are accompanied to all interviews if you wish
- See the statement document
- Appeal if dissatisfied

Summing up...

SENs covers a wide range of learning difficulties, and indeed, it can be suggested that it should include those with exceptional learning abilities. If your child does experience some learning difficulties, firstly, remember that many others are in the same boat.

Secondly, do take up the issues with the school, and if necessary the local education authority. Press your case firmly but politely if you feel you need to, and make sure that you get some independent advice from either a professional (social worker, doctor, solicitor, educational welfare officer) or a voluntary organisation, such as the Citizens Advice Bureau.

9 COPING WITH EXAMS

- Current qualifications
- How to deal with exams
- Keeping things in perspective
- Preparing for exams
- Revision techniques
- Exam entries
- Exam boards - how the system works
- Summing up...

The demands of the National Curriculum will mean that all students will have to face the stresses of examinations more frequently. In this chapter we will briefly look at the main types of qualifications school-age students take, and discuss the best ways to deal with the various problems posed by exams.

Current qualifications

Most students at schools in the UK will be prepared for GCSEs at 16.

Officially all grades of attainment at GCSE are considered to be 'passes', but in reality most employers will require grades from C upwards, as indeed will most schools when they are considering students wanting to study A levels.

The GCSE exam aims to cover the same levels as were previously tested by both O levels and CSEs, but the hope was that by having one exam the problem of 'second class' qualifications (CSEs) would be avoided. Many GCSEs include up to 20% coursework.

Students need careful guidance over coursework, as they may tend to leave it all to the last minute. Discuss this with your child's teacher and try to ensure that the task is broken down into several sections, with separate deadlines for each part of the project.

What happens after GCSE's?

After GCSEs students have several choices open to them if they decide to remain in full time education. Those who wish to continue a broad academic training can choose to study A levels, which will enable them to apply for a university place should they wish. A levels are generally seen as a difficult but prestigious exam, essential for university entrance.

Why take A Levels?

This view is gradually changing as the universities increase the number of places available. Nevertheless, A levels remain a good choice, since they are well respected, give the student a wide choice of universities, and keep career options pretty flexible. If your child enjoys traditional academic subjects and work, then A levels are probably right for them.

Vocational courses

Another option available now is the GNVQ (General National Vocational Qualification). These courses are more vocational in orientation, preparing students for broad career areas. So for example, a student could do a GNVQ in Health and Social Care if they were thinking of working in nursing, social work, or teaching.

There are GNVQs in many other vocational areas, eg Business Studies, Leisure and Tourism, Beauty, Catering, and Engineering. GNVQs can be taken at three levels; foundation, intermediate, and Advanced. Generally one would probably need about 4 GCSEs at grade C to get a place on a GNVQ Advanced course. It is possible to start at foundation grade and work up to Advanced grade.

GNVQ Advanced is acceptable to some universities, so GNVQ can be a good route to a university education for the student who does not want to take a traditional academic route.

How to deal with exams

Some people are remarkably immune to stress, and are not too worried by the prospect of exams. For most of us

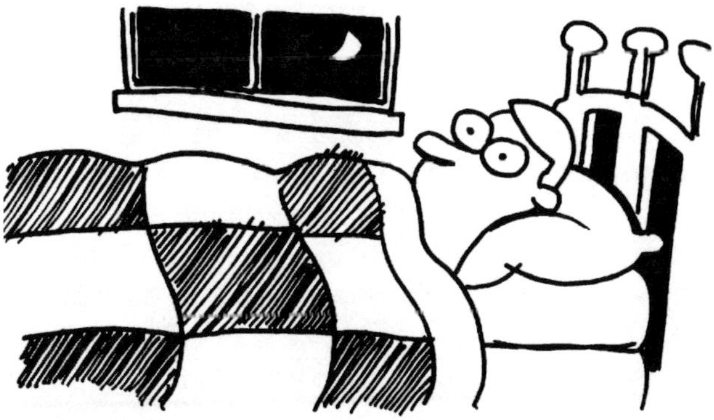

however, it is probably fair to say that the prospect of facing exams will cause us some degree of anxiety.

How well does your child cope?

For your child, learning to recognise their anxiety is the first step to coping with examination stress. Many people, perhaps well meaning, will emphasise the importance of doing well in exams. In many ways, this is right, because exam passes are important for future career choices.

However, for the child lacking self-confidence, this message can be a frightening one. Clearly, if a child is frightened at the prospect of exams, then they will not deal well with stress and may panic.

What is the best way to approach exams?

Other students may react with overconfidence, with equally disastrous results, either overestimating their abilities, or perhaps taking a relaxed attitude and believing that they will not need exam passes for their future plans.

Keeping things in perspective

The best approach towards exams, is to try to look at them in an unemotional, and down to earth way. Most of us would probably agree that it is no bad thing to get lots of A grades. Most of us would probably agree that we might feel a little put out by being told we are not quite as brilliant as we may like to feel we are. What we should remember is that exams are necessary for us to get on in life.

We shouldn't be overawed by the idea that a small group of students will always do better than us. It doesn't necessarily mean that they are better people than we are, or that they are always right. If we gain a B, C or D, it doesn't mean that we can never improve. An exam grade simply shows the level we achieved at a particular time.

Support and reassurance

Parents need to reassure their child that they shouldn't worry too much about other students. If they work carefully and consistently, they will almost certainly get their own share of the top grades. Above all, it is important to remember that everyone has both strengths and weaknesses. If your child is one of those lacking in self-confidence, it is probably worthwhile emphasising that last point; everyone has weaknesses.

Self-confidence

If you can help your child to develop their self-confidence and take this down to earth approach to their work and exams, they will have a good chance of passing their exams; and the grades will look after themselves!

Preparing for exams

Preparation is the key to ensuring exam success. Your child needs to acquire good study skills at an early stage and work consistently; last minute revision doesn't work.

Making a revision plan

- Revision for a GCSE or A level course needs to start early on in the course. Help your child draw up a detailed revision plan for the last six to nine months preceding an exam.
- Work needs to be reviewed on a weekly and monthly basis, perhaps starting with just an hour of revision per week.
- A good revision plan will be long-term, with regular reviews of progress.
- You will need to make sure that your child completes lots of practice exam questions - at home, and in addition to school work.
- Teachers may advise and be willing to look at extra work that your child does out of school.

Preparation

Preparing for exams is a bit like preparing for a sporting event. You need to make sure that your child has done the training, and that means knowing what they will have to do in the real event, being familiar with the number and types of questions which have to be answered.

Practice will make perfect, and it will mean that when it comes to the real event, your child will not be overawed by the occasion. It will be familiar to them, and they will know that they have to do something which they have already done many times before.

Revision techniques

The key thing to do when revising just about any subject is to make sure that you reduce the amount of factual knowledge that has to be remembered. There are lots of techniques which you can use to do this, eg:

- mnemonics
- rhymes
- Spider diagrams
- mind maps
- index cards

Students need to spend a lot of time reading and re-reading their notes and trying to boil these down to the most essential points.

Make revision active

It's vital though to make this a productive process, and that means short (about an hour) but frequent revision sessions. These sessions also have to be active. It's not helpful to simply look at notes with music blaring in the background.

Students can get someone (you, or a friend) to test them, or they might like to give you a brief lecture on a topic they have revised. Talk to them about the subjects they are revising. Ask them what they've learnt.

Exam entries

In most cases your child's school will pay examination entry fees and enter your child for the exam. Your child should receive some acknowledgement of their entry, which will include their candidate number and confirm the syllabus and the exam papers which they are sitting, and the date and time of the examination. Make sure that you and your child double check all these details, so that any mistakes can be rectified in plenty of time.

On the day

A few exam tips:

- Make sure your child is reasonably relaxed the day before an important exam. Some last minute revision is not a bad idea, but a very late night is not.

- Make sure they arrive at the school in good time for the exam. A few minutes early is a good idea, but a long wait will probably only set the nerves jangling.
- It can be a good idea to avoid friends and classmates just before and after the exam, especially if they are prone to winding up other members of the class.
- Needless to say, spare pens, pencils and other equipment are advisable. Nowadays students are allowed to take a variety of aids into exams, and it is wise to check with your school if you are in any doubt.
- A watch is one very important item which many students forget, but it is invaluable if your child is to use their time wisely.
- Food and drink are forbidden from the exam room, though a few mints can be helpful to calm the nerves for some, and most schools would probably not make an issue of it.

Exam boards - how the system works

Public examinations (GCSE's, A levels, and many of the vocational exams) are set and administered by Examination Boards, and are generally run in very similar ways.

The examiners

A Chief Examiner will be responsible for writing the exam questions and deciding how the exam will be marked. The Chief Examiner will have several Senior Examiners to help in this task. The Senior Examiners will all head teams of Team Leaders, who will in turn be responsible for up to about ten or so, Assistant Examiners.

The theory is that the Chief Examiner will define the required standard of work for all grades, and will ensure that all other examiners are in agreement as to how work will be marked and graded. At each level of the system, the examiners check each others marking, and this ensures that they all mark in the same way.

Positive marking

Broadly speaking, this system works very well. The rigorous system of cross checking means that many scripts are marked by two or even three examiners. All examiners' work is checked by another colleague. All examiners are required to mark positively, which means that they must reward students for what they have done, and not punish them for errors.

Can I appeal for a re-marking?

If examination results don't turn out to you or your child's satisfaction, it is possible to appeal against the decision of an examination board. You should bear in mind that if you appeal, you will have to pay a fee (about £20-£30).

In most cases it is the Chief Examiner who is personally responsible for marking scripts when appeals are made. You should also consider the fact that the grade given to re-marked scripts may go up or down - the Chief Examiner is entitled to change the grade in any direction.

Seek further advice

This means that you have to be very careful before deciding to ask for a re-mark. It is wise to seek the advice of the school before taking this step. It may be that the school is surprised by the results and will ask the exam board for a re-mark of all its students work. In this case you would not have to pay anything since it would be the school which was asking for a re-mark.

If your child was predicted pass grades and attained those in all other subjects, and one result sticks out as a glaring discrepancy, then it may be worth approaching the board, after seeking advice from your child's school.

Exam checklist

- Get a copy of the syllabus
- Find out exam details - time, place
- Check exam entry is correct
- Plan revision well in advance
- Allocate roughly equal time to all subjects
- Make revision active and frequent

Summing up...

Exams need to be put into perspective. For students who have followed their course carefully, exams are really fairly predictable. Students will mainly be summarising the work they have been doing in class under exam conditions.

Careful and consistent preparation should mean that your child is able to give an accurate reflection of their capabilities.

10 AFTER SCHOOL

- Lifelong education
- Planning for careers
- University education
- A year out
- Record of achievement
- References
- Summing up...

Lifelong education

Education no longer ends when your child has completed their secondary education. Education now has to be seen as a lifelong process, as many of us are likely to have to change jobs and gain new skills. Many people will undoubtedly wish to improve their prospects by continuing education, either by taking a degree course or gaining a vocational qualification.

This chapter will tell you about some of the key issues parents will need to be informed about to ensure their children continue to get the best from the educational opportunities available.

Planning for careers

Young people need to start thinking about their career interests towards the end of their secondary education, if not before. Many students can feel bewildered by the number of options available, or there may be an unwillingness or inability to think about such an important decision. Planning for a career needs, therefore, to be a long term project on the part of parents, students, and schools.

It is essential to give your child lots of opportunities to try out different types of work and explore different career opportunities. This can be done by work experience, shadowing, voluntary work, and using your local careers services.

What sort of person is your child?

Anyone trying to choose a career needs to have a clear and truthful picture of what sort of skills and activities they are good at, and what they enjoy. Self-knowledge is the key to getting the right career. Parents can help their child achieve this self-knowledge by providing ideas and opportunities to try various types of work.

University education

An increasing number of young people are studying a

degree course prior to seeking a job. A degree course is a good idea if your son or daughter is sufficiently qualified and feels that an academic education will be right for them.

If this is the case a degree in an academic subject, probably one which they have studied at A level, or are interested in, will give them a good general training. After this they can apply for jobs, and probably seek further job-related training or qualifications.

How to apply

If your son or daughter wishes to apply to university, you need to obtain a UCAS form and handbook (UCAS stands for Universities and Colleges Admissions Service - see Help List for details). Application is made the year before proposed entry, and you will have to pick six universities.

- You need to make sure that your child fully researches this issue.
- Students need to think carefully about what sort of course and university they want.
- Most universities have open days and it is a good idea to make use of these and see what the university has to offer.
- A great deal of care needs to be taken in compiling the UCAS form, and it is often helpful to photocopy the form and practice before finally completing the form.

Choosing Universities

There are two important issues to consider when filling the

form in.

- Firstly, your child should ensure that they know what sort of grade offers the universities they are applying to are likely to make. These should match your child's predicted A level grades.
- Secondly, you should ensure that at least a couple of your child's choices can be guaranteed to make lower grade offers.

This will mean that you have a lower offer to fall back on if your child doesn't obtain their predicted grades.

Other opportunities
If your child doesn't want an academic higher education, they will find a variety of opportunities for obtaining further qualifications, perhaps through an employer or a local Further Education college. Your local careers service will be able to give you full details of the opportunities in your area.

A year out

Some students going on to higher education like to take a year out of formal education. Many use this to travel and/ or gain useful work experience. If your child is interested in this idea, it is wise to check with the universities you are interested in and find out what their view of the 'year out' is. Some disapprove, but the majority are tolerant, especially if your child can prove that they have a well-thought-out and useful activity planned for the year.

Good ideas and bad ideas

Sitting on a tropical beach for a year would not be an impressive use of a year out in the eyes of most universities or employers. Voluntary work in Africa, or some type of work experience would be very impressive, indicating a lively, resourceful, and thoughtful character.

Check-list for University application

- Find out what courses are available.
- Find out what facilities universities have.
- Find out the typical A level grades required.
- Make a shortlist of 8 universities to select your final choice of six from.
- Make sure you will have a variety of grade offers, so that you have a reserve choice in case you don't get the grades for your first choice.
- Obtain a UCAS form and handbook from UCAS.
- Arrange to go to some open days.
- Talk to someone who has recently been a student, find out what it's like.
- If you are thinking of taking a year out, find out the universities' view of this. Make sure you have a clear plan of what you intend to do.
- Check with your local authority about applying for a grant. Estimate what you are likely to get and whether you will need

further support or loans.

- Investigate whether you can gain sponsorship for your course from an employer.

Record of achievement

The aim of the ROA scheme is that all students can complete their school careers with a folder which will demonstrate all their achievements during their school years. Whatever your child goes on to do after their school education it is a good idea to keep the ROA (and indeed all exam certificates) safely. Whatever critics may say of the ROA, it should provide a comprehensive record of what your child achieved at school.

References

At some stage your child will probably need to contact their school for a reference. It's worth remembering that while most teachers want to give good references to all their students, they are professionally bound to give an honest reference.

If a student has a poor attendance, punctuality, or discipline record, this will probably be reflected in some way in the reference. Obviously, it wouldn't be a good idea to pressurize your child with the threat of a bad reference, but it is a good idea to help them develop good timekeeping habits and to be polite and cooperative in dealing with other people, including difficult people.

Summing up...

Once your child has left school they will continue to need your support, though to a lesser extent. You can help your child prepare for the future by ensuring that they research the opportunities in further and higher education thoroughly, and get as much advice as possible.

Encourage your child to be critical in choosing a university or an employer - it needs to be their choice as much as that of a university or an employer if they are to be successful and enjoy their career.

...and finally

All the advice in this book boils down to a few key principles. If your child is to succeed in education they will need your support and encouragement. They will also need to reach a good understanding of their own abilities, to know their strengths and weaknesses, and what they enjoy most. If you can do anything to help your child achieve this sort of self-understanding and self-confidence, you can be sure that they will be well on the way to gaining the best start in life.

HELP LIST

- (i) Useful addresses
- (ii) Further reading

(i) Useful addresses

Appeals

The Secretary, Independent Appeals, Authority for School Examinations, Newcombe House, 45 Notting Hill Gate, London W11 3JB.
Tel 0171 229 1234.

Schools Curriculum and Assessment Authority (SCAA)

Newcombe House, 45 Notting Hill Gate, London W11 3JB.

SCAA Wales, Phase 2, East Buildings, Ty Glas Road, Llanishen, Cardiff CF4 5WE.

SCAA Northern Ireland, Rathgate House, Balloo Road, Bangor, County Down BT19 2PR.

DFEE

Sanctuary Buildings, Great Smith Street, Westminster, London SW1P 3BT.

DFEE: Welsh Office, Crown Building, Cathays Park, Cardiff CF1 3NQ.

DFEE; Northern Ireland (DENI),Rathgate House,Balloo Road, Bangor,County Down BT1 2PR.

DFEE Publications Centre, PO Box 2193, London, E15 2EU.
Tel 0171 510 0150.

British Dyslexia Association

98 London Road,Reading
RG1 5AU.
Tel 01734 668271.

Hyperactive Children's Support Group

71 Whyke Lane, Chichester, Sussex, PO19 2LD.
Tel 01903 725182.

National Association of Special Educational Needs (NASEN)

York House, Exhall Grange, Wheelwright Lane, Coventry, Warks CV7 9HP.
Tel 01203 362414.

Pre-School Playgroup Association

61-63 Kings Cross Road, London, WC1 9LL.
Tel 0171 833 0991.

Royal National Institute For the Blind

224 Great Portland Street, London W1N 6AA.
Tel 0171 3881266.

Royal National Institute For the Deaf

105 Gower Street, London WC1E 6AH.
Tel 0171 3878033.

Commission for Local Administration in England

'Local Government Ombudsman'
Greater London, Kent, Surrey, East and West Sussex.
Tel 0171 222 5622

The South West, the West, the South, East Anglia, and most of central England.
Tel 0123 695999

The East Midlands and the North of England.
Tel 01904 630151

There are separate Commissioners for Northern Ireland, Scotland, and Wales.

Your local council will be able to give further details.

Student Loans Company Ltd

100 Bothwell Street, Glasgow, G2 7JD.
Tel 0800 405 0100 (freephone)

UCAS (Universities and Colleges Admissions Service)

Fulton House, Jessop Avenue, Cheltenham, Glos. GL50 3SH. Applicant enquiries.
Tel (01242) 227788.

Associated Examinations Board

Stag Hill House, Guildford, Surrey.
Tel (01483) 506506.

Southern Examining Group address as above.

National Association For Gifted Children

1 South Audley Street, London W1Y 5DQ.

Citizens Advice Bureau

see local telephone directory for details.

Childline

Tel 0800 1111.

Independent Schools Information Service

56 Buckingham Gate, London SW1E 6AH.

(ii) Further reading

The Penguin Careers Guide

Anna Alston and Anne Daniel (1996)

The Daily Telegraph Schools Guide

John Clare, Ed. (Heinemann)

Jobs And Careers After A-Levels

Beryl Dixon (Hobsons Publishing, 1991)

All About The National Curriculum

C Emerson and I Goddard (Heinemann Educational Books, 1989)

The School Leaver's Handbook

J Grigg (Kogan Page, 1996)

Special Needs In Ordinary Schools

P Halliday (Cassell Educational, 1989)

Your Choice Of A-Levels

Hobsons Student Helpbooks/ CRAC (Hobsons Publishing, 1993)

Overcoming Dyslexia - A Straightforward Guide For Families And Teachers

B Hornsby (McDonald Optima, 1995)

Alpha To Omega The A-Z Of Teaching, Reading, Writing And Spelling

B Hornsby and F Shear (Heinemann 1980)

Matters Of Degree

Alan Jamieson (Hobsons Publishing, 1993)

The Reading Solution - Making Your Child A Reader For Life

Paul Kropp and Wendy Cooling (Harmondsworth, Penguin, 1995)

How To Complete Your UCAS Form

S Lainley and T Higgins (Trotman and Co)

Getting Into Vocational Qualifications

Katherine Lea (Richmond, Trotman and Co, 1993)

The Parents'A-Z

Penelope Leach (Harmondsworth, Penguin, 1983)

Assert Yourself

Gael Lindenfield (Thorsons, 1986)

CV's And Applications

Patricia McBride (Hobsons Publishing, 1994)

All About GCSE

M Mobley (Heinemann Educational Books, 1986)

A Guide To The National Curriculum

Bob Moon (Oxford University Press, 1994)

Getting Into Oxford Or Cambridge

MPW (Richmond, Trotman and Co, 1994)

The Good Study Guide

Andrew Northedge (Open University Press, 1990)

Bullying

V O'Donnell (Attic Press, 1995)

Parenting Teenagers

Make the Most of this Unique Relationship
Polly Bird ISBN 1-86144-018-9
£5.99 120pp Pub Sep 96

Parenting Teenagers is the answer to all parents' prayers - a comprehensive guide to helping make the 'teenage years' in any household as pleasurable as possible. Packed with information, advice and tips, *Parenting Teenagers* is aimed at anyone who has the task of bringing up teenagers - parents and carers. It will also be of interest to those who work with teenagers such as teachers, social workers, youth leaders and so on.

A Parent's Guide To Dyslexia And Other Learning Difficulties

Maria Chivers ISBN 1-86144-026-X
£6.99 128pp Pub June 97

Learning difficulties are slowly being specified and recognised, and medical and educational help developed. To get this help for your child you need to know how to make the system work for you. Maria Chivers draws on expert knowledge to show how you can make this happen. This guide takes you step by step through diagnosis, treatment, education, and beyond into career options.

The World's Your Oyster

Education and Training for Adults
Polly Bird ISBN 1-86144-014-6
£5.99 110pp Pub July 96

A complete guide to education and training for adults. The number of mature entrants to higher education in the UK in 1993 was up by 128% on 1982.

Starting School

Lyn Cartner ISBN 1-86144-031-6
£6.99 100pp Pub July 97

Starting School takes you through the process of primary school entry, tells you what to expect and suggests how you can deal with commonly occuring problems. It will help you and your child prepare for the changes school will bring.

A Parent's Guide To Drugs

Judy Mackie ISBN 1-86144-028-6
£6.99 108pp Pub June 97

Whether you suspect your child, or their friends, may be taking drugs, or are simply worried by the horror stories and headlines - this practical guide will take you through the facts and basic steps, which you can use and develop to suit your own circumstances.